First published by AuthorHouse 01/05/06

ISBN: 1-4259-0136-0 (sc)

Library of Congress Control Number: 2005910781

Printed in the United States of America
Bloomington, Indiana

Cover illustration by Dan Larsen

This book is printed on acid-free

1663 LIBERTY DRIVE
BLOOMINGTON, INDIANA 47403
(800) 839-8640
www.authorhouse.com

Dedication

This book is dedicated to all the parents,

siblings and grandparents

who have lost a baby due to

Sudden Infant Death Syndrome.

Forward

This story was written by the babysitter who found Hannah in her crib on Valentine's Day.

It was written to help children understand the feelings and thoughts of a little girl who lost her sister. Its message will help parents tell the story of Sudden Infant Death Syndrome (SIDS) to children in a simple way.

Along with the children who contributed pictures to illustrate this book, many others helped to make its publication possible.

Children are Forever

Diamonds in the rough,
these precious babes of mine,
created in the Father's Plan
before the sun did shine.

You've given us this task, Lord,
to cut and shape these stones,
until beneath their earthly crust,
the Light of Christ has shown.

Use these anxious hands, O Lord,
give them your control,
help me chisel out the facets
still unknown.

When their life is over,
and they come before your throne,
may these precious diamonds be
a reflection of your own...

Darlene Kane
November, 1978

Missing Hannah

Based On A True Story of Sudden Infant Death

by

Darlene Kane

Hi!

My name is Katie.

I'm 5 years old.

I'm going to have a baby sister.

Ashleigh Welko

My Mommy and Daddy are so excited.

Me, too!

I tell everyone I meet that we are
going to name her Hannah.

Emily Kuhn

I went shopping with Mommy for Hannah.

We bought clothes, diapers
and lots of stuff.

Mommy's friends gave her a shower
(that's when they buy things for the baby).

3

Daddy fixed up Hannah's room.

He painted and put up some pictures of Winnie the Pooh and Tigger.

I like Tigger, he is so <u>bouncy</u>!

I like the yellow walls.

Mommy and I went to see Dr. Davis.

She weighed Mommy and listened to Hannah's heart beat through her stethoscope.

She took a picture of Hannah in Mommy's tummy. It looked funny!

Francia Harris

Grandma and Grandpa came over today and brought me a puzzle.

Grandpa says I'll be a Super Sister.

I think so too!

6

I like to jump rope.
I hope Hannah does too!

I will bake her cookies.
I will read Hannah stories.
We will have tea parties under this tree!

I love Hannah!

...I skip a lot.

Francia Harris

My mommy reads me stories about babies. She tells me all about me.

I was a cute baby and I didn't cry a lot. I smiled and smiled and everyone thought I was pretty.

My eyes are blue. My hair is brown. Sometimes I have freckles when the sun shines on my face.

Amanda King

When I got up this morning, Grandma was fixing me some cereal. She said Mommy and Daddy went to the hospital to have Hannah.

Would I like to go see her?

Oh, YES, Grandma!
Let's go NOW!

9

Jessica Morton

We drove to the hospital. It was big. We went up the elevator to the floor where Mommy was staying.

Daddy was so happy to see me. He picked me up and showed me Hannah in the nursery room. She is SO little.

Daddy said Hannah weighs 7 pounds, 8 ounces and is 19 inches long.

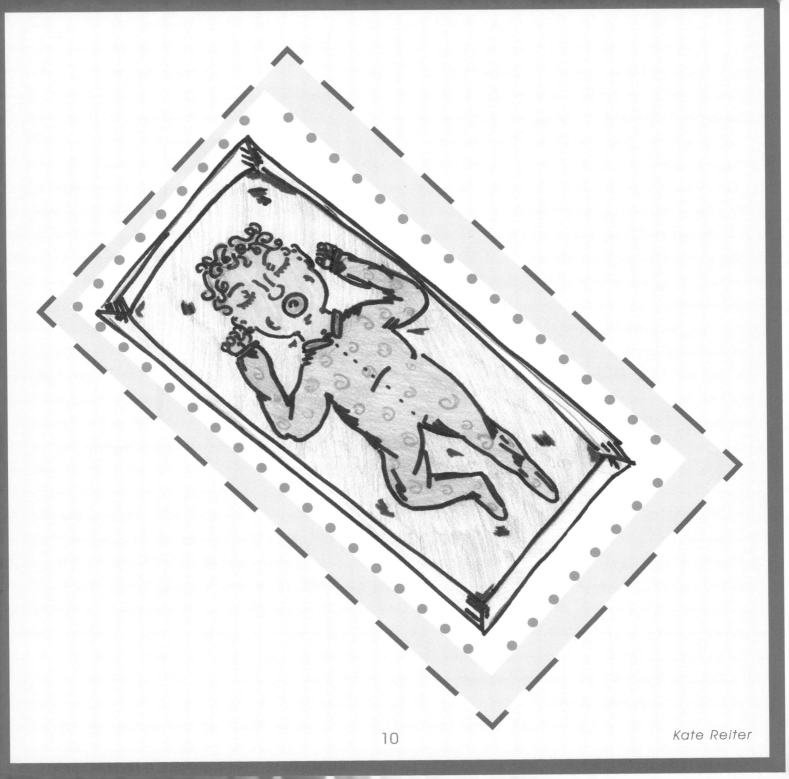

10

Mommy's room was very pretty. The yellow flowers Grandma and I sent were on her window sill. She had another lady in the same room who had a baby boy. They talked and talked about babies.

Mommy looks very happy.

I am happy too!

Allison Salmons

Today Mommy came home with Hannah and I got to hold her in a big chair.

I was a little afraid when I was holding her. I gave her a bottle of milk and she liked it.

She sleeps a lot!

Emily Kuhn

Mommy and I took Hannah
for a ride in her stroller.
I got to push it.

We went to the store and
to grandma's to visit.

Everyone is so happy!

Jacqueline Massary

Hannah cries more now that she is bigger. I think she is funny when she cries.

I talk to her sometimes and she listens to me. I tell her about jumping rope and tea parties under the big tree.

Doctor Davis gave Hannah a checkup. She said Hannah now is 13 pounds and 22 inches long.

She is very healthy and pretty soon she will be eating baby food.

It will be fun to feed her!

Ashley Lazo

This is Valentine's Day! Mommy and Daddy are going out for a special dinner. Carrie, our babysitter, is coming over.

I like her a lot! She reads me stories and lets me stay up and take care of Hannah.

This time Carrie helped me make a special Valentine's card for Hannah and put it on her bedroom wall.

When I woke up today Mommy and Daddy were crying. Grandma and Grandpa were crying too.

They said Hannah went to the hospital last night.

She stopped breathing.

I cried too.

17

Emily Kuhn

The doctors said Hannah died of SIDS.

What is SIDS, Mommy?

No one knows much about SIDS.
Some babies die while they are sleeping.

Can I die while I am sleeping?

Mommy says I am too old to die from SIDS.

Katie Rose

We went to the funeral place where Hannah was in a small box. People came to look at her and tell Mommy and Daddy how sorry they were for us.

Lots of flowers were around Hannah. She looked very nice.

People cried. I cried.
I kissed Hannah goodby.
I put the valentine in her hand.

I love you Hannah. I miss you.

Katie Rose

I sometimes sit under my big tree in my backyard and pretend to have a tea party with Hannah.

I jump rope and pretend Hannah is jumping with me.

I talk to Hannah too.

Lindsay Smith

Mommy and Daddy read a lot about SIDS in books from the library.

Mommy is going to a meeting with other mothers who lost babies, too.

Mommy told me it helps to cry and talk about Hannah.

I hope Mommy has another baby soon.

Laura Bailey

Mommy hugs me a lot.

Grandma kisses me a lot and
Daddy picks me up and tells me
I am pretty.

Rachel Harris

Hannah's room is closed. I go inside sometimes and play with Hannah's toys and talk to her.

It makes me feel happy when I play in her room.

It makes me feel sad too.

I sometimes cry.
I miss Hannah.

23

Jessica Morton

I drew this picture.

I will always love you Hannah.

I am sorry that you died.

I wish you didn't.

I miss you Hannah.

Jennifer Prosise

Sometimes Mommy, Daddy and I go
to the cemetery where
Hannah is buried.

I put pictures on Hannah's grave
and Mommy puts flowers.

We talk to Hannah and tell her
all about our tea parties.

Maureen Farris

Acknowledgments

I gratefully acknowledge the friendship, support and encouragement so freely given by my family and friends.

I also thank Sister Marilyn and her students at Our Lady of the Elms (Akron, Ohio) for their fine art work.

Also, I thank Dan Larsen for his cover design and Susan E. Jones for the layout design of *Missing Hannah*.

About the Author

Darlene Kane wrote *Missing Hannah* based on an experience in her life. While raising her three children she also operated a day care business for 29 years. It was during this period that a child she was caring for suddenly died. Reflection on the tragic death and the impact on the other children involved resulted in *Missing Hannah.*

The book has been several years in the making. The illustrations were created by children at a local grade school. This was a result of her relationship with teachers and students at the school. The involvement of children in the creation of the book seemed very natural. Darlene was born and educated in the Cleveland, Ohio area. Prior to her 35 year marriage she studied religion in Cincinnati, Ohio. Her spiritual background and love for children resulted in a caring relationship with many children and their parents over the years. She hopes that *Missing Hannah* will provide help to children that are involved in the tragedy of an infant death.

Printed in the United States
88224LV00002B